Songs of

the heart

Songs of the heart

VERSE I
A Chartus.X anthology

Edited by
Xyvah Okoye and Ezgi Gurhan

SONGS OF THE HEART
Verse I: A Chartus.X Poetry Anthology
Paperback ISBN: 978-1-915129-27-7
eBook ISBN: 978-1-915129-28-4

This collection published in 2023 by Chartus.X
www.chartusx.org

Proofed by Caitlin Miller
Typeset by Ezgi Gürhan

Images from canva.com

Content Warning

This book features elements of self-harm, strong language and sexual content.

Contents

Foreword

As one of the rawest forms of writing, throughout history, poetry has been a way of self-expression. It is a medium that allows the heart to sing and the soul to soar.

In the creation of this anthology, *Songs of the Heart*, I have had the privilege of curating a collection that captures the joys and lamentations dwelling within the poets' souls. These verses range from personal experiences to social issues that stir our souls and ignite a fire within us against the injustices we endure.

Working on this anthology alongside Xyvah Okoye has been a transformative journey for me. It has boosted my confidence and helped me realise that I possess the ability to create something meaningful, both as a poet and an editor.

For me, writing poetry has been a rocky journey. Years of being subjected to restrictive literary analysis in school left me with little understanding or appreciation for this art form. I perceived it as a writing style reserved for the snobbish, those who couldn't enjoy the beauty of prose. The same people who dismissed genre fiction as "not real literature," sneered at popular culture, ridiculing anything and everything fictional and magical.

It was not until I discovered poetry as a cathartic form that I truly understood its power. It became a means for me to purge the swirling emotions that threatened to overwhelm me. I vividly recall writing my first poem right after my High School graduation ceremony, slightly tipsy and compelled by an urgent need to pour my thoughts onto paper.

If I had to name a poet who shattered my preconceived notions, transforming my perception of poetry from an archaic, rule-bound medium to a liberating art form, that would be Nikita Gill. Her verses taught me that writing poetry can be an act of liberation. That is what poetry essentially is to me today. It allows me to break free from feeling trapped and angry at the world and within myself.

With this anthology series, I aspire to accomplish for others what Nikita Gill's poems did for me. I want to reshape people's opinions on reading and writing poetry, challenging the notion that it is a boring or intimidating experience. I want readers to immerse themselves in the songs of our hearts that we have meticulously collated and refined in *Verse 1*, and in doing so, I hope they find the inspiration to compose their own opus.

I extend my heartfelt gratitude to the poets whose voices grace these pages. Their words have enriched our lives, reminding us of the resilience, beauty, and power inherent in the human experience. I also extend my gratitude to you, the reader, who is embarking on this poetic journey with us. As you read this anthology, may the songs of our hearts reverberate within your soul, inspiring you to embrace the transformative magic of poetry and compose your own symphony of liberation.

- Ezgi Gürhan,
Editorial Assistant

Hannah Olesen

She is a twenty-four-year-old writer who has a couple of articles published but hopes to publish something creative.

A Puzzle Piece

To fit inside a puzzle piece
I'd wonder where I'd go
Would I travel the world?
Or make a home?

To fit inside a puzzle piece
I'd never need a mask
I'd never need a hat
Or clothes that fit right

To fit inside a puzzle piece
Would finally set me free
I'd throw away my mirrors
I'd yell my name at passersby

To fit inside a puzzle piece
I'd never need my mind
To play this board game
That lives inside their eyes

Chocolate Smile

I never told you that,
You had chocolate stuck in your smile

Your laughter made birds sing
And I was tired of the silence
I didn't want to ruin it with such a critique
I wanted you to remember it like a movie
No blooper reels or scene breaks
Our crisp moment that needed no change
I took the check before you put it on credit
And then the sun set bouncing off the car window

We went on about the pastel cardigans
You clutched your chest like you had pearls
And bragged about the maid that had a separate house
I, the butler who opens the door and
You, the Queen who tips me a penny
Laughing till our stomachs cried

That's when I could see that,
You had chocolate stuck in your smile

Marilyn

I want to say her
But I'm not her
Surrounded by men
She was loved, not learned
Most famous woman
Asked about a man
What kind of wedding?
What attracted you to him?

Did no one know

Or were they happy,
By her never-ending beauty…

Barely said happy
Never asked why
Only why him

I wish I could say her
But I didn't know her
I don't think anyone did
But I'd ask her why
Not why him
And then I'd tell her

Goodbye

Nicolina Ashby

Nicolina Ashby enjoys a good walk and writing experimental fiction, such as combining horror and comedy in abstract ways. When it comes to poetry, however, she tends to have a bias towards representing tough human experiences. Loneliness, depression, and loss, for example, are all themes she likes to explore.

Lone Spirit

It can see the masses,
Who are themselves blind,
No chance for them
To grant its find,

Through Shanghai it wisps,
Like an old paper bag,
Gone like the wind,
As though cursed by a hag,

Alone and afraid and anxious at life,
What could be more a miserable sight?
Surely not, the dog with no stick?
Surely not, the hopes about to get the kick?

Such answers, the spirit won't get,
'Hello to nature and her heart divine,'
In death they've returned back to that state,
When will that freedom truly be mine?'

Patricia Mercado

Patricia Mercado is a Creative Writing and Publishing MA student. She loves finding different ways of portraying deep emotion—how it can change and wreck us physically—through words. She hopes to one day reach a lot of people through poetry and be able to remind them that there is nothing wrong with feeling everything and nothing all at once.

A Sign Of Weakness

It was not easy, reaching this place.
Even now, I fear I have made a mistake,
slipping in between the rough torrent.
Tell me then, is it over, these breaking of bones,
the water shaping itself to solid and
I'm back in the four-corner room,
across from you, you hold no shame.
Under your gaze, my ribs break
into itself, collapsing into a cave.

I lay quiet. Living but not breathing
in this stillness. I cannot find you
and I still struggle to hear you.
Forgive me, Lord, for I have sinned.

Have I made it?
Doubt is a white hand clawing.
Am I ungrateful?
Sin is a white flame burning
through flesh.
Am I worth saving?
I keep waiting for something
to change, for you to find me.
Or perhaps I have become
infertile soil
and it is in your plan.

Air is water
I panic.
My head breaks the surface
and my hands find enough marshy
land to drag myself through.
Swallowing is painful, tides of emotion
forcing my body to break open
And in my hands, I hold my own heart.

Without thinking, I swallow it.
Without thinking, I want to live.

Freya Thorne

Biotechnologist, artist, poet, and reader Freya Thorne likes to explore the themes of trauma and dark emotions in her writing.

When She Fell Apart

When it rained in her world
it fell on her tear-stained face,
washing away the last of her tears.

When the freezing stormy wind blew,
they brushed her skin,
and took away with them,
his fingers' traces.

When it thundered,
it shielded her from criticising, judgemental screams,
and reminded her, *never to lose faith in herself again.*

When lightning struck,
it gave her strength and courage,
to patch up her shredded tapestry
and walk out of the storm.

So she arose through the storm,
Carefully, avoiding the sharp edges of her past.

As she finally stood up,
the stars shone brightly,
transforming the harsh darkness into a peaceful starry
night.

Starlight gave her hope and confidence,
encouraging her to start over,
to redesign a new path for a brighter, happier future.
And when the soothing breeze stroked her hair,
It silently whispered,
May you have the power to rise above every storm in your life.
And even louder:
Never forget that without discouragement and hardships,
you never could have - *So fearlessly and cannily,*

by choice or some magnificent fierce coincidence -
arrived here.

Leaving behind the pain, the hurt,
In the fading storm,
She finally began to move on.

Change

Smile for a while,
lay back a little.
Don't bring those tears back,
'Cause they don't make your eyes glitter.
Lie on the floor,
and forget about the world
Don't open your eyes
till the bitter feeling goes.
Pain will slowly disappear,
you just have to let the time pass.
Don't hurt yourself for those
who broke your heart.
You stand strong alone,
Don't need to wait for anyone to hold.
Never fail to trust yourself,
You are braver than anyone else.
Forget the past,
But don't forget its lessons.
People will come and go,
that's what life is all about.
Don't chase the ones
Who wish to run away.
But do claim the ones
Who are not afraid to stay.
And at last,
Smile while it lasts,
and cry when it ends.
But don't you break down now,
Cause your life is yet to start.

Search for Happiness…

She has lost her way,
In the darkness she used to stay.
Been in the dark for too long,
Can't bear the light now.
Used to being all alone,
don't remember what it felt like to be someone's someone.
Happiness has faded,
friends have become strangers,
relationships are scattered.
And the wounds on her thighs have become deeper and wider.
Faith is shaken, trust is broken,
everything which was once so close
has now gone so far.
Wounds of her past hunt her down,
She doesn't want to leave the shadows now.
Tears have turned to bloodstains,
She has become numb to blade,
Has become numb to pain.
Survival is all she has learned
from all that she has suffered.
Lost in the hurtful memories of her past,
tell me how she will find her happiness now?

Rachel C. Hyde

Rachel C. Hyde is a novelist with an unhealthy addiction to coffee and chocolate eclairs. She lives with her husband and dog in the not-so-sunny seaside town of Worthing. Her biggest dream in life is to have a novel published - her second biggest dream is to one day own a very expensive coffee maker.

Hyde has a BA in English Lit and Creative Writing and is currently completing an MA in Creative Writing and Publishing. When not crying over her laptop, she can be found walking her dog by the sea, combing charity shops for books, or rewatching Gilmore Girls for the gazillionth time.

City Nights

Cocktail bars and fairy lights,
Painted faces and drunken plights.

We see the city in a smoky haze,
Dancing, laughter, smiles for days.

Kisses under star-filled skies,
Hands on skin, fingertips on thighs.

We love, we lust, we live the night,
Young, mad, and free until sunrise.

Lady Chaos

Greedy as Sin, pretty as Death,
She tells lies with a hand over her chest.

She doesn't want love, she loves only War,
She prays to the Devil, and he answers her call.

She'll kiss you with her eyes open, she'll stab you with a smile,
She's greedy as Sin, pretty as Hell.

Huntress

Beneath a blanket of dark and glitter
there stalks a woman smiling at the night
Eyes bright and misty, her skirt short and tight,
she knows what she's hunting; eager, young lover
Prowling concrete jungles – silent hunter,
Smoke, glowing lights, and thudding music heart-
beats as she makes seduction look an art,
a dance, a kiss, she's both siren, woman…other.

Another predator wrapped in silk, yet
for all the thrill of whisky-tainted skin,
for all the pleasure of cherry red lips.
The love she chases - love she won't forget,
Is her romance with the night sky and sin,
with the dark and her city made of bricks.

Exquisite

Suck my lip 'til it's sore,
Scratch my skin 'til it's raw,
You're an exquisite kind of pain that I've never known
before.

Bite me and tear at me,
Swallow me Hole,
You're the most exquisite pain that I have ever known.

Consume my body,
Purple my soul,
Heal me with the most exquisite words that have ever been
told.

Push me away and pull me back,
Shield me from the light,
Then shower me with rain and the most exquisite lies.

Take me in and tire me out,
Stretch my body, lay me down,
Bury me with flowers and the most exquisite crown.

The Moon-Quiet Boy And The Sun-Bright Girl

She's got a mouth full of secrets and danger in her eyes,
She's got a fire in her soul and a tongue that tells only lies.

He is the calm before the storm, the quiet in the night,
His thoughts are like snow, while his smile brings the light.

Together they are eternal – sea brushing against sand,
He is moon-quiet and strong, she sun-bright and grand.

Together they are jigsaw pieces sliding neatly into place,
She would move the worlds for him, he would shower
stars upon her face.

The Bridge

We are building bridges that were broken
over rivers that we filled with wild waters -
don't look down.

We are pushing for the future
while trying to avoid, avoid the past -
don't look back.

We have forgiven but not forgotten
we do not have the means or the words to say
we're "sorry" or "you were wrong" -
don't speak now.

The bridge is fragile, fragile, fragile
but strong enough to hold
we can reach the other side
if only we let go
…
…
…
Tiptoe, tiptoe.

A Collection Of Parts

My head is
spilling, spilling, spilling,
cluttered with ideas,
notebooks half-
filled,
cups of tea half-
drunk.

My heart is
filling, filling, filling,
daily phone calls with my mum,
collecting friends like stamps,
rings on my finger,
vows easy to make.

My body is
broken, broken, broken,
a temple, unreliable but strong,
sliced open, stitched together,
threadbare patchwork doll,
just an envelope for a soul.

My voice is
loud, loud, loud,
scrambling for the words to say
everything, everything, everything,
all of it, all of it
my own.

Ezgi Gürhan

As a writer, poet, and avid reader, she is interested in narratives of female experiences, mythology, fairy tale retellings, and all things fantasy.

Second Best

Always second best
Alone and disposable

Never important enough
To cause a thought

A doll, a possession
Without true value

A commodity,
A decoration

Always there,
So very dependable

Absolutely gullible
With no pride nor merit

Not compared to him
The idiot

Born first, born a man
No other talent than that

A great feat indeed
To survive without a brain

Applaud him, break her,
Neglect her, dote on him

It's not like she'll ever leave
She is truly that
Fucking
Stupid

The Fool

To play a fool
Day and night

Don't offend,
Just play along

Laugh it off,
Save the drama

I hear, I see,
I understand

I am no fool
Without a thought

I see you,
Your jealous
Venom

Sinking in
To maim and
Break

Turn the other cheek,
They say.

Let yourself be hurt
Better that than hurting others

Be a good person,
Polite and thoughtful.

Let them devour your soul
Little by little
Day by day

Maybe, one day,
When nothing is left

When you become the powerless
Fool they want so bad
All will truly be well.

Before,

When nothing
truly mattered.
All was glossed over.

Back then,
it was easy
simple,
uncomplicated.

Lies and superficial
relationships
were hidden
behind a veil.

Now the truth is
Out—out in the open,
under the great
shimmering light.

Friendships
without depth
are seen
as they are.

The City Lights

The city lights always sparkle,
Making the world bathe in yellow lights.
I watch them,
And I think about what it was like before there was
electricity,
Before there were so many street lamps.
Was the world swallowed up by darkness?
Did people walk down sombre alleys,
Where dangerous shadows lurked?
Perhaps it was ugly and unsafe.
Yet, perhaps it was prettier and more mysterious.
Perhaps, back then, none were afraid of the dark.

Moving on

Run away, far, and far
Until the point of start
Is no longer seen

Leave it all behind
Those times of old
Where null was right

Forget the pain
Forsake the past

Let time start anew

Build it up high
This gleaming life
Of dreams.

Empty House

A flickering light at
The end of the hall

Not a soul in sight
Just the hollow silence
Of an empty house

Did time freeze
While I was out?

Had everything
Finally disappeared?

Everything I wished to
Be gone,
Now no more…

Their Shallow Words

And worthless opinions
Are of no consequence.

As long as you know who you are
And approve of yourself,
Knowing yourself to be right and good,
Nothing truly matters.

All those who judge and belittle you
Are merely minor details,
Tiny footnotes
No one will ever remember,
Glance at, or even notice.

Xyvah Okoye

Xyvah Okoye is an epic fantasy author and believer.

When she isn't tinkering with the mechanics of another story, she might be refuelling her magic in a pool, on the beach, or close to some other body of water. And at times like that, with her pointy ears twitching and her button nose buried in a book, if you look close enough, you just might see the shimmering veil around her… The veil between this world, and hers… Between what is, and what possibly could be.

To find out more, visit www.xmokoye.com

Before I Sleep

I sit and I watch as my life passes by
I gleam and I stare and I glare
Those who hate me and spite me have taken my joy
And those who love me aren't near.

One said I should write when I feel so unhappy
So I'm writing my feelings to you
I sit and I sob and I stare so sadly
Because I don't know what else to do.

I feel really dejected, it hurts me so bad
As the thoughts keep coming to my head
I never knew gain came with such pain
And I think now I will go to bed.

Ever Since I Met You

Though we haven't been the best of friends
I really thought you should know
How you made me feel deep inside

You made me feel like I was meant to protect you
Like you were my property
Like I was your bodyguard
You made me feel so insecure
So unsure of what steps to take

You made me wonder if things
Could ever go smoothly between us
You made me feel jealous of your friends
That they were so close to you

You made me angry with myself
For all I did to you, good or bad
You made me regret the days
I made you laugh

You took away my pride
You made me forget
What was the most important
The most essential to me

I loved you, I really did
I tried my best to please you
To make you happy
I now feel
Maybe I tried too hard
Maybe I stressed you that way

I don't want us to grow apart
Though we never really were near
I care for you

I care about you
I fear to lose you
I fear to give you up

To friends, to foes, to life
And most of all, to death
I don't want to hurt you
I don't want to hurt me

I really still do and always will
Have a soft spot for you
Deep down inside me
Deep down in my heart
You will always remain special to me
You will always be in my heart

That Foolish Act

One silly little act
I will live to regret
Has a silly little fact
I will never forget

My sharpener had a blade
The thought swelled in my head
The silly move I made
Could nearly have me dead

My heart felt very heavy
My head felt in the stars
But now I pay the levy
'Cos now I see the scars

My hand was very soft
The blade was shining bright
I held the blade aloft
The move I made that night

The blade now seems so cruel
The thought keeps coming back
I went into a duel
The blade just had a snack

And no one really knows
Why I did all these things
I wish I had a prose
To talk about these things

The times I felt real sad
The pain could almost kill
But now I feel real bad
I would have paid that bill

I just can't hide the tears
It kills me deep inside
'Cos all my worst of fears
I now have brought to light

My sleeves drawn to my fingertips
To conceal the terrible sight
The bloodstained blade below now drips
That foolish act that night

A Letter To A Lover

You know,
It's been so long since we last met
Since I felt you close to me
Since I heard your soft voice whisper,
"It's alright."
Long since I last felt your skin touch mine
And your breath upon my neck
And your lips upon my ear, nibbling gently,
Softly, steadily
Long since I tasted your breath
Long since our eyes met
And we were under the tranquil trace, so tacit
When last were we locked in a kiss?
I remember vividly those cold nights
With you by my side to keep me warm
To hold me and love me all through the night
When again shall I feel that protection?
When again shall I feel that comfort and sanctity
Of being part of you, and you of me?
I can't wait anymore
The nights barren with cold fast approach
And I need you to keep me warm
To derive great joy from the fun midnight games we played
To feel your hands across my skin
To feel your body press closely upon me
To feel your fingers run through my hair
Down my face, my neck, my body, my thighs,
To feel that you love me
To feel that security, that affection
To know you are always there
My love, my friend, my all.

My Eutopia

Why can't I stop to breathe
Without thinking about you?
What have you done to me?
I can't seem to get your face
Out of my head
It's so confusing
Yet, I like it

I like the fact that
No matter where I run
No matter where I hide
I can't escape you
To come to join you

But how I wonder
I'd love to come, love to be
With you forever and ever
You inside me and me inside you
But how? How can this happen
When there's no link between
My real world and you
My Eutopia?

Too Much Like You

I'm too much like you to hate you
I'm too much like you, I fear
I'm too much like you to hate you
And that's how I know you care
When in life you find a reason
And that reason's never clear
Then I know I cannot hate you
The only thing I hate is fear

Life goes up, life comes down
And there's no one around
In the cold and frosty nights
I can hear in my sleep
All the times that you weep
And you cast the tears from sight
In the cold and dark of night

You helped me
And you showed me the reasons
Why I cry in the night
I watched you sleep
I heard you weep
For the sins of my world
For a boy, for a girl

I'm too much like you to hate you
I'm too much like you, I fear
I'm too much like you to hate you
And that's how I know you care
When in life you find a reason
And that reason's never clear
Then I know I cannot hate you
The only thing I hate is fear

Heroine East

Amateur writer & student who enjoys twisting
words until they make you feel something.

Oh Stop

2:32 from bringing him to me.
Endless tussling in the sheets. falling. floating. landing in his
dreamland.
Desperate. creasing. unspoken. urges. can't keep count of
every time
I cave in.

older. crooked teeth. heavy. longing. stare.
Delicate hand in just the right places.
silver rings. tattooed. into his skin.
They're taking mine. braiding us
back together.

Oh.
Still so pretty.
shirt. navy. unbuttoned. chest. hair.
Not my ring hanging from his neck.
we're not vowed but
woven.
woven hearts.

twirling around in the warmest lights. in the whitest night.
hanging by a thin, thin thread. on the thin, thin ledge.
of fir and pine and fragile ornaments
and we don't look down, down there
or else
the spinning
will
slowly
come
to
oh
please.
stop.
Stop him from twisting the bedsheets.

I roll away.

barefoot. lonely. pillow. couch. where that man does not
snore.
I can bring myself back. back to last Christmas. back to
that tree. back to hanging by that thin, thin thread. and we
we would
exist again
for at least two more hours
before work.

Tal Rejwan

Writer, artist, reader, and dreamer Tal Rejwan has previously illustrated the cover for *Creel 5* and the Hebrew editions of the *Tear Asunder* series by Nashoda Rose. After working at Graff Publishing as a social media manager, she decided to pursue her long-life dream of becoming an author and taking on a bigger role in the publishing industry. She completed a Creative Writing BA at The University of Essex and is currently studying a Creative Writing and Publishing MA at Kingston University.

Make me cry

One more time
Curled toes and hot breath
A trickle of sweat
Running down, down,
My spine
Cold and foreign
To the coals of mine
round apple to the ground
Splash,
Make me cry.

Tender.
My skin is tender to the touch
You make it tender,
With edge
slicing wind,
your embrace as I inhale
Softly
With bite of rope and
Roving hands
The tense of tiny nerves
Tighter bind
between my thighs,
around my neck,
Make me cry.

Read to me

Read to me.
Part the pages
With a finger,
Then two
Lick the tip,
Smudge the ink
Spread it
Yes,
Smear it,
Make a mess
With your words
With the markings
On the page.

Read to me
Words of poets, lovers, writers.
Yes, read them.
But your words?
Whisper them
In my ear, to my core
Hiss them,
Roar them,
Scream them,
Never read.

Speak directly to my aching cunt
Slow burn of desire
Shot inside
Make my legs cross,
The fabric cling,
Silk, slick, stick
My skin

Say heat,
Say soft,
Say fast, hard, weep.
Say
Deep.

More, read to me more
And when all the books are
Gone,
And it's just you and me
Alone.

Turning leaves

You can attach a
String
To harness a
Kite

You can bottle up
Water
To quench your
Thirst

But you can never
Catch
The change of
Autumn

Stop the leaves from
Turning
Their vivid colours
Crimson

As you can
Never tame
nor subdue
me

Desire

Peak of light
Shine so bright
The undercurrent wave
Washes through the
Cave

Pleasure, leisure, measure
How far will I go
Let go
Go,
Go!

A cage of comfort
A call from the wild
Torn, worn, gone
How far can I go?
The hands who feed
The hand that
Gives

Clipped wings
Adorning crown
Will she stay
Will she drown

The only thing I learnt in life
Desire is undesirable
But desire
Is life

Tamar

Curved bells like teardrops
Hanging from their spine
The Bluebell is so lovely
Fairies hiding within its petals
And next to it is a sign,
Do not pluck or harm!

The Catchfly, so dainty
Elegant and sweet
Waking up to say hello
In wintertime
And next to it is a sign,
Do not pluck or harm!

The Centaury blushing pink
So shy and meek
But oh, so mighty
Just ask your local witch
And next to it is a sign,
Do not pluck or harm!

Round five-leaved
Grows in the cold
Yet, kissed by sun
Is the Cinquefoil flower
And next to it is a sign,
Do not pluck or harm!

From July to August
A rare little one indeed
Deep pink petals dotted
Is the Deptford Pink
Next to it is a sign,

Do not pluck or harm!
But next to the little garden pansy
There is no warning sign
So she could only wish to grow
Sharp thorns and wits

And if I were a flower
Maybe I had a chance
And if I were a flower
Maybe you wouldn't pluck.

Yiran Wei

Yiran Wei, from China. She is a student majoring in creative writing and has published poetry in the "English and Chinese Romantic Dictionary."

Piercing Through

Nibbling at a toe is the lark,
Quietly turning away is the brown lizard,
Facing you
you blue my eyes.
I delve in...
Exploring your purple throat—
It is the dawn.

Who is clenching their nails?
It's a young colt,
Rabbit's long ears pressed against your protruding navel.
You are a whale making way for the cloud.
You are a sigh the colour of maroon.
Your fragile bones,
Pinned, pinned,
Pinned inside a watery coffin.

How did you grasp the inner wall of my heart?
How did you control my knees and barriers?
Your skills, unlike a towering building suddenly rising,
Nor like a white crane passing through a mountain's crev-
ice...

You never incited the white grapes to moan and swell until
they burst the iron wine cup.
And your delicate eyelashes, like the spring rain, are not
axes.
They have not parted heaven and earth.

Legendary Realism

That night,
the heavy snowfall sealed the city.
The snowflakes' gears.
Once again devoured the skin.
It also beat the blood and alcohol senseless.
At that time,
fortune stood on the cliff, choosing to end their own life.

As for me,
On the same bright day,
I raise my pen again and write in Mandarin,
Like lifting a destiny, I cannot choose.
The metaphorical sentence dissipates like fog.
I evade language,
As if evading a black spell.
Rainbows, roses, or a withered heart,
Become the damp fuse of a bombshell.
Doubt, then, becomes a kind of skin—
A visible pore is everywhere.

I've tried asking for dreams, escape, drugs, and all the
creatively erotic postures.
I asked, stumbled, fallen or through deserts and withered
trees.
Do we still need to be loved?
Where should we go?

...

Our legal other half is hanged on the crescent moon,
right?
They silently recite poems.
And poems grow arms and eyes…
Which nationality do poems become?
If we invert A,

Will the high tower become a ruin?
And the circle, O,
Is it a cycle of false alarms?
Ghosts gather in a circle and dance and revel all night.
Fortune stands on a bright cliff, choosing to end their own
life.

Signposting to Support Services

If you're struggling with your mental health and need support, we highly recommend that you speak to your doctor, GP or any of the professional services listed below.

Mind
www.mind.org.uk
InfoLine: 0300 123 3393
The Mind InfoLine can help you find specialist services in your area.

Samaritans
www.samaritans.org
24 hours a day, 365 days a year. Call 116 123 (free from any phone).

Shout
www.giveusashout.org
For immediate support text SHOUT to 85258 to chat by text to a trained and supervised volunteer. Free, confidential, and available 24 hours a day, 365 days a year.

For more options, visit the Helplines Partnership website
for a directory of UK helplines:
www.helplines.org/helplines

Meet the Editors

Xyvah Okoye

An anime-watcher and booklover, Xyvah exists in multiple worlds at once. She considers this to be a good thing, especially when she needs a break from her stressful part-time job of being a functioning human being. That being said, music and chocolate do a great job of getting her through the day.

Outside of being a person, Xyvah is the founder and Executive Director of Chartus.X Publishing, a UK-based independent publishing company, where she works with writers and affiliates to produce outstanding books and authors. She also offers independent coaching, providing information, templates, encouragement and tailored guidance on writing and publishing to aspiring and already-published authors.

She has worked on a range of titles, from children's books to adult nonfiction, giving a platform to underrepresented and marginalized voices in the industry.

Xyvah spends most of her time building worlds, writing stories and drinking coffee.

Ezgi Gürhan

Before coming to work as an editor for the Verse poetry anthology series, she was the Editor-in-Chief for the publication of *Creel 5: An Anthology of Creative Writing*, which made her decide to study for a Master's degree in Creative Writing and Publishing at Kingston University to learn how to create more and more books to unleash into the wilderness we call the world.

About Chartus.X Publishing

Founded August 2020, Chartus.X Publishing is a UK-based independent publishing company giving platform to diverse and marginalized voices around the world. We believe in the power and importance of books, and we believe great stories deserve to be heard.

As a publisher, we strive to put out original, high-quality content at fair prices, while quick-stepping to the fast-changing market and adapting in the ways necessary to get our stories heard. The company is run by a team of authors and business individuals working in tandem with other industry professionals.

Currently, three imprints exist within Chartus.X LTD:

1). Chartus.X Publishing - imprint for fiction and non-fiction across board.

2). Two Trees Books - imprint for young adult Sci-Fi and fantasy.

3). Six Bricks Publishing - imprint for all middle grade & children's titles.

At Chartus.X, we believe it takes all types to make a world, and so we are accepting of everyone, no matter our differences. Being a writer is a journey with many twists and turns along the way. Our team is dedicated to making that journey a memorably pleasant one.

9 781915 129277